10 STEPS TO MAKING REAL FRIENDS

A comprehensive guides on how to attract, make friends, be confidence and have influence on people

Patience John

Copyright © 2024 by Patience John

All rights reserved

No part of this book may be reproduced, stored in a retrieval system, or transmitted, in any form or by any means, electronic, mechanical, photocopying, recording, or otherwise, without the prior written permission of the author, except in the case of brief quotations embodied in critical reviews and certain other non-commercial uses permitted by copyright law.

This book is a work of non-fiction. The names, characters, places, and incidents are products of the author's imagination or are used fictitiously. Any resemblance to actual events, locales, or persons, living or dead, is entirely coincidental.

TABLE OF CONTENT

INTRODUCTION
The Importance of Genuine Friendships

So I called Peace my best friend instructing her to go to my house and help me do something, really!! At first I thought she will decline, I had to use some bucks to bait her or should I say to bribe her into performing the task for me as I wasn't in town.

Guess what! She decline accepting money from me and chose to help me for free even though she had to leave her office to go get it done. I said to myself 'who wouldn't want a real friend around them, someone to easily rely on. Friendship is like a cosy blanket that wraps us in warmth, joy, and a sense of belonging in life's busy chaos. Real friends are like steady guides, offering support, understanding, and company when we need it most. They're the folks we lean on in tough times, the ones who reflect our true selves, and the hands that lift us up when life gets tough.

True friendships are built on a foundation of authenticity – a genuine acceptance of each other's flaws, celebrating successes, and sticking together through life's ups and downs. Unlike fleeting connections, real friendships grow stronger with time, deepening with every shared experience and heartfelt chat.

But what makes real friendships so special? It's the feeling of acceptance and belonging they give us – a safe space where we can be ourselves, share our worries, and find comfort in the company of kindred spirits. It's the laughter that echoes in our hearts, the tears shed together, and the quiet moments that speak volumes without words. Important of friendship and why you should thrive to make one for yourself.

Let me tell you about Lily and Rose, childhood pals who weathered life's storms together, sharing secrets and adventures along the way.

Lily and Rose had been friends from childhood, their friendship formed throughout their youth and cemented by the challenges of maturity. Despite life's ups and downs, they remained confidantes, comrades, and partner in crime so to speak.

One summer afternoon, while sitting at Rose's bedside in the hospital, Rose, who was fighting a terrible illness, was feeble and weak, her spirit dampened by the weight of uncertainty and worry.

In those times of calm togethemess, Lily realised that true friendships weather any storm. They are the lifelines that hold us together when life's storms threaten to overwhelm us, the lighthouses that lead us through the night, and the sweet whispers of hope that remind us we are never alone.

As Lily grasped Rose's hand, she silently promised to treasure their relationship and nourish it with love, laughter, and everlasting support and to stick together in time like this one. She discovered peace, strength, and the timeless beauty of genuine human connection in the tapestry of their shared experiences.

The story of Lily and Rose serves as a painful reminder of the value of real friendships, demonstrating their significant influence on our lives and the lasting legacy they leave behind.

In this book, we'll dive into the heart of true friendships: what makes them tick, the perks they bring, and how they can change our lives for the better. Through stories, insights, and practical tips, we'll unravel the threads that bind us and discover the beauty of genuine human connection

STEP 1
Understanding the Essence of Real Friendship

Let's dig into what makes real friendships so important. Real friendships aren't just about casual hangouts – they're built on honesty, trust, and having each other's backs. They're like a safe space where you can be yourself without worrying about being judged.

Here are some key things that make real friendships special:

Trust: Real friends trust each other with their secrets and struggles, knowing they can rely on each other no matter what.

Loyalty: True friends stick together through thick and thin, supporting each other through tough times.

Empathy: Real friends understand and care about each other's feelings, offering a shoulder to lean on when things get tough.

Acceptance: Genuine friendships accept people for who they are, flaws and all, celebrating what makes each person unique.

Respect: Real friends treat each other with kindness and respect, listening to each other's opinions and boundaries.

Real friendships can have a big impact on our lives. They're like a warm hug when we're feeling lonely, a listening ear when we're unsure, and a cheerleader when we succeed. They encourage us to be our best selves and make us feel happier and more connected overall.

These are the reasons you need to look out for a real friend and to cherish the friendships – they're not just nice to have, they're essential for our well-being and happiness.

Defining genuine friendship

Understanding what makes real friendship special is really important when you're trying to make true friends. Real friendship goes beyond just saying hello or being casual buddies; it's a strong bond built on being real, trusting each other, and respecting one another. Knowing what real friendship is all about is the starting point for building friendships that last.

Real friendship starts with being honest and sincere. It's about being open and sharing both the good and tough times, and accepting each other just as we are. Unlike those surface-level friendships, real friends are comfortable being vulnerable and expressing themselves without worrying about being judged.

Trust is super important in real friendships. Real friends know they can share their secrets and weaknesses without fearing they'll be spilled. Trust is the solid ground real friendships stand on, making the connection strong and dependable.

Supporting each other is another big part of real friendship. Real friends stick together through thick and thin, giving each other encouragement and help when it's needed most. They're there to listen, lend a hand, or simply be there for each other through life's troubles.

Respecting each other is key in real friendships too. Real friends are nice, kind, and respectful of each other's thoughts, boundaries, and independence. Respect makes communication smooth and helps everyone understand each other better.

Lastly, real friendship is like a two-way street where both sides care about each other. It's about putting in the time, effort, and care to grow the friendship and support each other along the way. Real friendship brings happiness, camaraderie, and a sense of belonging to our lives.

Understanding these special qualities of real friendship is crucial if you want to build true friendships. By being genuine, trustworthy, supportive, and respectful in our relationships, we create meaningful connections that make life richer and more fulfilling.

Exploring the benefits of authentic connections

To form real friendships, it's important to understand the many good things that come from making genuine connections. Genuine connections aren't just about surface-level chats; they're meaningful bonds that make our lives better in lots of ways. Let's talk about the different benefits of building these real connections and how they make us feel happier and healthier.

Emotional Support: Genuine connections give us a strong support system for both good and tough times. Having friends who genuinely care about us can give us comfort, reassurance, and understanding when we're feeling stressed, sad, or lost. Knowing we have someone to rely on can make us feel less alone and more secure.

Increased Happiness: Real friendships bring happiness and fun into our lives. Sharing experiences, jokes, and heart-to-heart talks with friends can lift our mood and make us feel good inside. Genuine connections create happy memories and make us feel more satisfied and fulfilled.

Enhanced Mental Health: Making real connections is good for our mental health. Research shows that people with supportive friends are less likely to feel depressed or anxious. Genuine friendships make us feel valued, accepted, and understood, which helps us feel better about ourselves.

Increased Sense of Belonging: Real connections make us feel like we belong. Feeling connected to people who share our interests and experiences makes us feel like we're part of a group. Genuine friendships let us be ourselves without worrying about being judged, which makes us feel accepted and included.

Opportunities for Growth and Learning: Real friendships help us grow and learn new things about the world and ourselves. Talking to friends with different perspectives and experiences helps us see things in new ways and try new stuff. Genuine connections encourage us to step out of our comfort zones and explore new hobbies and experiences, which helps us grow as people.

Longer, Happier Lives: Genuine friendships can help us live longer and happier lives. Research suggests that people with strong social connections tend to be healthier and live longer. Real friends provide support, encouragement, and inspiration during tough times, helping us stay strong and positive through life's challenges.

STEP 2

Building Self-Awareness for Meaningful friendships

To build strong friendships that last, it's crucial to know yourself, and that's what this chapter is all about. Let's talk about why understanding who you are is so important when it comes to connecting with others. When we explore our thoughts, feelings, and reasons behind what we do, it sets the stage for more meaningful and genuine connections.

Understanding yourself means recognizing and getting why you feel the way you do, what you believe in, your strengths, and even your not-so-great parts. It's about thinking about yourself, looking inside, and honestly figuring out who you are and what makes you tick. Getting self-aware helps us to notice the patterns in how we act, understand why we react in certain situations, and see how our actions affect the people around us.

Why self-awareness is a big deal in friendships

Being Real: When you know yourself, you can be genuine in your interactions. Understanding your beliefs, likes, and where you draw the line helps you share yourself honestly with others, building true connections based on openness and truth.

Feeling Others: Self-awareness helps you understand and share the feelings of others – that's empathy. Knowing your emotions makes it easier to get where others are coming from, making your connections stronger and creating mutual understanding.

Sorting Out Conflicts: Knowing yourself is crucial for fixing problems in friendships. Understanding your triggers, biases, and how you talk helps you handle disagreements better. Being self-aware helps you handle conflicts, control your emotions in a good way, and find solutions that work for everyone.

Growing Personally: Self-awareness is like a superpower for growing as a person. When you see your strengths and weaknesses, you can find areas to improve and actively work on being the best version of yourself. Real connections act like mirrors, showing you where you can grow and giving you helpful feedback to get better.

Here are some easy ways to get more self-aware and build better friendships:

Mindfulness: Try simple things like meditation or writing in a journal to pay more attention to your thoughts, feelings, and how your body reacts. It helps you understand yourself better.

Ask for Feedback: Talk to your trusted family, or mentors and ask for their thoughts. Good feedback gives you useful insights into how others see you and helps you find areas to get even better.

Think About Your Past: Spend some time thinking about your past experiences, friendships, and how you acted. Figure out how these things shaped your thoughts, values, and actions, and what you can learn from them.

Discover Yourself: Try activities like personality tests, thinking about your values, or answering self-reflection questions to learn more about who you are, what drives you, and what you want to achieve.

Reflecting on your own values and qualities

In this section, we'll talk about why it's important to look inside to understand your own values and qualities. Knowing what matters to you and what makes you unique sets the foundation for building real and fulfilling friendships with others. Let's explore how thinking about your beliefs and traits can help you handle situations and connect with others on a deeper level.

Understanding Your Values: Think about the ideas and beliefs that guide how you act and make decisions in life. They shape what's important to you, your goals, and how you deal with the world around you. Taking time to think about your beliefs helps you figure out what matters most to you and what you stand for. Knowing your values helps you connect your actions with what you believe, which makes your interactions more honest and real.

Identifying Your Qualities: Your qualities are the things that make up your personality. They include your talents, weaknesses, personality traits, and little quirks that make you who you are. Thinking about your qualities helps you understand yourself better and how you behave in friendships. Recognizing your strengths lets you use them to make your connections with others better. And knowing your weaknesses helps you focus on areas where you can grow and get better, which helps you learn more about yourself.

Self-reflection gives you insight into your values and how they affect friendships. By thinking about your experiences, behaviors, and how you interact with others, you can spot patterns, see things from a different perspective, and make smart choices for the future. Reflecting on yourself also helps you pay attention and think about things more deeply, so you can be more present and focused in your friendships.

Reflecting on your values and qualities can happen in lots of ways, like:

- *Writing in a Journal*: Write down your thoughts, feelings, and experiences about your values and qualities. Use prompts or questions to help you think and discover new things about yourself.

- **Meditation**: Try mindfulness meditation to clear your mind and pay attention to your inner thoughts and feelings. Notice how your values and qualities show up in your thoughts and actions.

- *Asking for Feedback*: Talk to people you trust, like friends, family, or mentors, and ask them what they think about your beliefs and qualities. Their thoughts can give you helpful ideas and help you see yourself better.

- *Making Time for Reflection*: Set aside regular time to think and reflect on things. Find a quiet spot where you can think without distractions, so you can really explore your values and qualities.

Thinking about your own beliefs and qualities can help you understand yourself better and build more meaningful and genuine relationships with others. As you start on your journey of self-discovery, take the chance to learn what makes you special and build connections that celebrate the real you.

Understanding your social needs and preferences

To make strong connections, you first need to know what you want and like in social situations. This section looks at why understanding your needs and preferences in social interactions is important for building real connections with others. Let's see how knowing your social needs and preferences can help you handle meetings and build better connections.

Know Your Social Needs:

Social needs are what you desire and need in relationships, like friendship, support, understanding, and belonging. Knowing your social needs helps you figure out what's important for your well-being and happiness in your relationships. Understanding your social needs lets you look for interactions that meet those needs and focus on connections that make your life better.

Identify Your Social Preferences:

Social preferences are the kinds of interactions and activities you enjoy and feel comfortable with in social situations. They include things like the size of gatherings, how close you want to be in relationships, how often you want to hang out with others, and what kind of things you like doing with friends. Knowing your social preferences helps you feel confident and real in social situations, so you can find environments and relationships that fit with what you like.

Why Knowing Your Social Needs and Preferences Matters:

Knowing your social needs and preferences is important for a few reasons:

1. *Makes You Happier*: Recognizing and meeting your social needs makes you feel better and happier overall. Having relationships that meet your social needs gives you support, lowers feelings of loneliness, and helps you feel like you belong.

2. *Helps You Be Yourself*: Knowing your social preferences lets you be yourself in friendship without

pretending to be someone you're not. Being true to yourself and what you like lets you build real connections based on understanding and respect.

3. Helps You Choose Relationships: Knowing what you need and like in relationships helps you pick the right ones to focus on. It lets you look for connections that match your beliefs, interests, and lifestyle, so you can have relationships that are meaningful and make you happy.

Ways to Understand Your Social Needs and Preferences:

1. *Think about Your Past*: Reflect on your past experiences with relationships and think about what made you feel good and what didn't.

2. *Talk about It:* Be open with yourself and others about what you want and like in relationships. Share your thoughts and feelings with people you trust and listen to what they have to say.

3. *Try New Things*: Be open to trying different social activities to see what you like and don't like. Pay attention to how different situations make you feel and adjust your social interactions based on what you learn.

Knowing your social needs and preferences helps you handle relationships better, be more confident, and be yourself. As you start to understand yourself better in social situations, may you find connections that respect and enhance who you are.

STEP 3
Cultivating Empathy and Compassion

This chapter explores the importance of nurturing empathy and compassion to create meaningful connections. Understanding and connecting with others on a deeper level is facilitated by empathy and compassion. Let's delve into how nurturing these traits can enhance our connections and cultivate deeper relationships with others.

Exploring Empathy

Understanding and sharing the feelings of others is a key aspect of empathy. Understanding involves empathising with others, seeing situations from their point of view, and feeling their emotions deeply. Nurturing empathy helps us build authentic connections with others, leading to trust, understanding, and mutual respect in our relationships.

Embracing empathy

Showing kindness, understanding, and support to others, especially during challenging times, is essential. It requires being there for others, lending an ear, and giving support and help when necessary. Cultivating compassion allows us to offer support and encouragement to those around us, creating a sense of warmth and belonging in our relationships.

The Benefits of Empathy and Compassion

Cultivating empathy and compassion offers numerous benefits for both ourselves and others

Enhances Connection: Empathy and compassion deepen our connections with others by fostering understanding and empathy. They enable us to build trust and rapport, creating a safe and supportive environment for open communication and vulnerability.

Fosters Emotional Resilience: Empathy and compassion strengthen our emotional resilience by allowing us to navigate difficult emotions and experiences with grace and understanding. They provide a source of comfort and support during challenging times, helping us feel less alone and more capable of facing adversity.

Promotes Conflict Resolution: Empathy and compassion are essential for resolving conflicts and disagreements in relationships. By understanding and validating each other's perspectives, we can find common ground and work towards mutually beneficial solutions, fostering harmony and cooperation.

Cultivates a Culture of Kindness: Practicing empathy and compassion creates a culture of kindness and generosity in our relationships and communities. It inspires acts of generosity and selflessness, promoting a sense of unity and solidarity among individuals.

Practical Strategies for Cultivating Empathy and Compassion

Active Listening: Practice active listening by fully engaging with others and seeking to understand their thoughts, feelings, and experiences without judgment or interruption.

Perspective-taking: Make an effort to see situations from the perspective of others, considering their feelings, beliefs, and motivations when interacting with them.

Kindness and Generosity: Show kindness and generosity towards others by offering support, encouragement, and assistance whenever possible.

Self-Reflection: Reflect on your own thoughts, feelings, and behaviours, and consider how they impact others. Identify areas where you can improve your empathy and compassion towards others.

By cultivating empathy and compassion, we can create deeper and more meaningful connections with those around us.

Practicing active listening and empathy

Active listening and empathy are essential in the process of creating meaningful friendships. Let's look at why actively listening to people and demonstrating empathy are important in the process of developing genuine relationships.

Active listening is about completely connecting with others when they talk, concentrating on comprehending their meaning rather than simply hearing their words. To understand what they're saying completely, you must pay attention to their tone, body language, and emotions. By actively listening, we demonstrate respect for their opinions and feelings, which promotes trust and openness in our interactions.

Empathy is intimately linked to active listening. It is about understanding and sharing the feelings and experiences of people. Empathy enables us to connect with others on a deeper level by noticing and validating their emotions. When we display empathy, we indicate that we care about their well-being and are available to help them through lives up and downs.

Practicing active listening and empathy provides various benefits in our desire to develop genuine friends:

Enhanced Understanding: Active listening and empathy allow us to better grasp others' viewpoints, feelings, and experiences. This shared understanding promotes respect and strengthens ties.

Strengthened Bonds: By actively listening and empathising with people, we may foster trust and rapport in our connection. When individuals feel heard and understood, they are more willing to open up and reveal their true ideas and feelings, which strengthens our relationships with them.

Conflict Resolution: Active listening and empathy are essential for resolving disagreements and misconceptions. By listening empathetically to all parties and understanding their sentiments, we may discover common ground and strive towards a peaceful resolution.

Emotional Support: By actively listening and demonstrating empathy, we may give emotional support to our friends at difficult times. When we affirm their feelings and listen without judgement, we provide a secure environment in which they may express themselves and seek comfort and reassurance.

Practical Tips for Active Listening and Empathy

- Give your pals your undivided attention while they speak, making eye contact and avoiding distractions.
- Listen without interrupting or developing a response while they speak.
- Reflect on what you've heard to verify comprehension and affirm their emotions.
- Empathy is demonstrated by acknowledging their emotions and providing support and understanding.
- Allow your friends to fully express themselves without hurrying or judgement.

Note that active listening and empathy are necessary for building genuine friends. By actively listening to people and demonstrating empathy, we encourage an environment of trust, understanding, and mutual respect, which are the building blocks of meaningful friendships.

Nurturing compassion in your interactions

In the goal of making real friends, nurturing kindness in your relationships is key. Compassion includes understanding, love, and kindness towards others, and it forms the bedrock of real connections. Let's dig into why fostering compassion in your conversations is crucial for making real friends and how it adds to important relationships.

Compassion is the ability to notice and react to the suffering and needs of others with empathy and kindness. It includes actively trying to understand the experiences and feelings of others and responding in a supportive and caring way. When you develop kindness in your relationships, you create a caring environment that supports trust, understanding, and real connection.

Here's why nurturing kindness is important in making real friends

1. *Cultivating Understanding*: Compassion pushes you to actively listen and empathize with others' feelings and emotions. By knowing their views and feelings, you build stronger relationships based on mutual respect and care.

2. *Creating Supportive Relationships*: Compassion creates an environment of support and encouragement in your relationships. When you show kindness and understanding towards others, you create a safe place where they feel valued and accepted, setting the basis for true bonds.

3. Building Trust: Compassion improves trust and rapport in your interactions. When you constantly show empathy and kindness towards others, they feel more comfortable opening up and sharing their thoughts and feelings with you, strengthening the bonds of friendship.

4. Encouraging Reciprocity: Nurturing kindness in your relationships promotes reciprocity and mutual support. When you show compassion towards others, they are more likely to respond and give support and understanding in return, creating a positive cycle of kindness and connection.

Practical Ways to Nurture Compassion in Your Interactions.

1. *Show Empathy*: Put yourself in others' shoes and try to understand their viewpoint and feelings. Validate their thoughts and offer support and guidance.

2. *Practice Kindness*: Show acts of kindness and giving towards others, both in words and deeds. Small acts of kindness can make a significant difference in developing compassion and making relationships.

3. *Be Genuine*: Approach your relationships with sincerity and truthfulness. Show genuine interest and care for others' well-being, and be ready to give support and assistance when required.

4. *Cultivate Patience*: Be patient and understanding with others, especially during difficult times. Practice patience and tolerance, and try to keep a positive and helpful mood in your encounters.

STEP 4
Initiating Meaningful Conversations

Initiating meaningful talks is a basic step in the path of making real friends. In this chapter, we'll explore the value of meaningful talks and how they serve as bridges to building genuine relationships with others. Let's dig into why initiating important conversations is crucial for making real friends and how it adds to the formation of lasting relationships.

Meaningful conversations are the building blocks of real relationships. They provide opportunities to share ideas, feelings, and experiences, allowing people to connect on a deeper level. Unlike superficial interactions, meaningful talks promote understanding, empathy, and mutual respect, setting the groundwork for genuine friendships to bloom.

Here's why starting meaningful talks is vital in making real friends

1. *Fostering Connection*: Meaningful talks build a sense of connection and closeness between people. When people participate in open and honest conversation, they create rapport and trust, forging bonds that transcend superficiality.

2. *Cultivating Understanding*: Meaningful talks help individuals to share their views, beliefs, and experiences. Through active listening and empathetic involvement, participants gain insights into each other's lives, creating mutual understanding and respect.

3. *Building Trust*: Meaningful talks build trust and sincerity in partnerships. When people feel heard and understood, they are more likely to open up and share their vulnerabilities, increasing the level of trust and intimacy between them.

4. *Discovering Common Ground*: Meaningful talks provide chances to discover common hobbies, beliefs, and experiences. As individuals participate in dialogue, they discover commonalities that serve as the basis for genuine friendships.

Practical Tips for Initiating Meaningful Conversations

1. *Be Genuine*: Approach talks with authenticity and truthfulness. Share your thoughts, feelings, and experiences freely, and encourage others to do the same.

2. *Ask Open-Ended Questions*: Encourage deeper talks by asking open-ended questions that prompt thought and analysis. Avoid yes/no questions and instead, ask questions that invite explanation and study.

3. *Share Personal Stories*: Share personal stories and experiences that help others to get to know you on a deeper level. Vulnerability creates connection, so don't be afraid to share your thoughts and feelings genuinely.

4. *Respect Differences*: Approach talks with an open mind and a desire to learn from others. Respect differences in views, beliefs, and experiences, and participate in conversation with curiosity and respect.

Breaking the ice and overcoming social anxiety

In the quest to make real friends, breaking the ice and beating social anxiety are critical steps towards building lasting relationships. This chapter discusses the significance of beating social obstacles and nervousness, and how doing so creates paths for genuine relationships to develop. Let's dive into why breaking the ice and overcoming social anxiety are important for making real friends and how they contribute to building authentic relationships.

Breaking the Ice: Initiating Conversations with Confidence and Ease

Breaking the ice includes starting conversations and engaging with others in social situations. It's about taking the first step towards bonding with people and building rapport. For many people, starting talks can be daunting, especially in new or group settings. However, breaking the ice is important for creating chances for meaningful exchanges and bonds to grow.

Here's why breaking the ice is important in making real friends

1. *Creates Opportunities for Connection*: Breaking the ice opens the door for important talks and interactions to take place. By starting talks with others, you create chances to get to know each other and build shared ground.

2. *Builds Confidence*: Initiating talks helps you build confidence and social skills. With practice, you become more comfortable engaging with others and navigating social settings, which improves their ability to make authentic connections.

3. *Promotes inclusion*: Breaking the ice promotes inclusion and a sense of belonging in social settings. By starting talks with others, you make everyone feel welcome and respected, creating a positive and inviting atmosphere for friendship to grow.

Practical Strategies for Breaking the Ice and Overcoming Social Anxiety

1. *Start Small*: Begin by starting conversations in low-pressure situations, such as casual social gatherings or group settings with friends.

2. *Pay attention to them*: Focus on actively listening to others during talks, rather than thinking about what to say next. This helps ease social anxiety and develops authentic connections.

3. *Challenge Negative Thoughts*: Challenge negative thoughts and beliefs about social interactions by rewriting them in a more positive and realistic way.

4. **Seek help**: Reach out to family members, or mental health professionals for help and advice in overcoming social anxiety and building confidence in social settings.

Friendships unfold, enriching your life and the lives of those around you

As you start on the journey of making real friends, it's important to understand that friendships have the power to enrich our lives and the lives of those around us. This heading dives into the profound effect of authentic connections and how they contribute to personal growth, happiness, and a sense of belonging. Let's explore why relationships unfold and how they bring fulfilment and joy to our lives, staying true to the spirit of making real friends.

The Beauty of Genuine Connections

Genuine ties form the backbone of important interactions. They are defined by authenticity, trust, and mutual respect, creating a feeling of camaraderie and understanding between people. Unlike superficial encounters, genuine relationships pierce the surface and touch the hearts and minds of those involved.

Here's why relationships develop and improve our lives

1. *Personal Growth*: Genuine friendships provide chances for personal growth and self-discovery. Through interactions with others, people gain new views, insights, and experiences that broaden their horizons and improve their knowledge of themselves and the world around them.

2. *Emotional Support*: friendships offer a source of emotional support and comfort during both happy and difficult times. Genuine friends stand by each other through thick and thin, giving a shoulder to lean on, an ear to listen, and a hand to hold when needed most.

3. *Shared Experiences*: Genuine relationships are built on shared experiences, memories, and times of laughter and joy. These shared experiences build ties that withstand the test of time and form the basis of long friendships.

4. *Sense of Belonging*: Genuine Friendship promote a sense of belonging and respect. They build groups where people feel valued, understood, and admired for who they are, regardless of their backgrounds or differences.

5. *Mutual Growth and Learning:* Friendships provide chances for mutual growth and learning. Through open conversation, teamwork, and shared experiences, individuals learn from each other, push one another, and inspire each other to be the best versions of themselves.

Embracing the Journey of Making Real Friends

Making real friends is not just about widening our social groups; it's about developing authentic relationships that improve our lives and the lives of those we chose to keep as friends. It's about being vulnerable, open, and real in our interactions, and enjoying the beauty of human connection.

As we manage the complexities of friendship, let us cherish the relationships that unfold, noting the profound impact they have on our well-being and happiness. Let us develop empathy, kindness, and sensitivity in our encounters, and nurture the bonds of friendship with care and purpose.

In the path of making real friends, may we enjoy the beauty of genuine connections, and may our lives be enriched by the meaningful relationships we form along the way.

STEP 5
Being Authentic and Vulnerable

In the aim of developing true friends, embracing sincerity and vulnerability is vital. This chapter addresses the necessity of being truthful and vulnerable in building meaningful relationships and fostering true connections. Let's look into why honesty and vulnerability are crucial factors in forming true friends and how they contribute to the depth and sincerity of our relationships.

The Importance of Authenticity

Authenticity is about being honest to oneself and expressing genuine ideas, feelings, and beliefs without pretence or veneer. It entails accepting one's strengths, shortcomings, and defects and enabling people to see us as we actually are. Authenticity forms the cornerstone of true connections, encouraging trust, intimacy, and mutual respect in relationships.

Here's why sincerity is key in developing actual friends

1. *Building Trust*: Authenticity develops trust between individuals, creating a safe and secure setting for open and honest conversation. When we are authentic, others feel comfortable being themselves around us, knowing that they are welcomed and cherished for who they are.

2. *Fostering Genuine ties*: Authenticity develops genuine ties based on mutual understanding and acceptance. When we show up as our true selves, we attract like-minded folks who resonate with our beliefs, interests, and objectives, leading to deeper and more lasting interactions.

3. *Enhancing Self-Awareness*: Being truthful enables us to have a better knowledge of ourselves and our relationships. By embracing our real selves, we become more self-aware, understanding our strengths, limitations, and places for progress, which helps to personal development and self-improvement.

The Power of Vulnerability

Vulnerability entails the willingness to exhibit our genuine selves and share our thoughts, emotions, and experiences honestly with others. It demands bravery and honesty, as it includes taking chances and venturing outside of our comfort zones. Despite its apparent hazards, vulnerability is a motivator for true connections and emotional closeness in friendships.

Here's why vulnerability is vital in developing meaningful friends

1. *Fostering Emotional Intimacy*: Vulnerability develops emotional intimacy by offering opportunity for true connection and understanding. When we allow ourselves to be vulnerable, we welcome people to share in our experiences and feelings, developing friendship and empathy.

2. *Cultivating Trust and Empathy*: Vulnerability cultivates trust and empathy in friendships by exhibiting honesty and sincerity. When we share our vulnerabilities with others, we make room for compassion and understanding, strengthening the foundation of our interactions.

3. *Encouraging Mutual Support*: Vulnerability enhances mutual support and reciprocity in partnerships. When we expose our vulnerabilities, we urge others to do the same, establishing a culture of support and empathy where individuals feel valued and understood.

Practical Strategies for Being Authentic and Vulnerable

1. *Practice Self-Reflection*: Take time to think on your values, beliefs, and emotions, and explore how these impact your interactions and relationships.

2. *Cultivate Self-Acceptance*: Embrace your strengths, shortcomings, and defects, and enjoy the unique aspects that make you who you are.

3. **Encourage Open Communication**: Create an environment of open communication where honesty and vulnerability are encouraged and accepted.

4. *Build Trust Gradually*: Allow trust to emerge organically over time by being consistent, reliable, and real in your relationships.

STEP 6
Navigating Conflict and Resolution

Conflict is an unavoidable element of human interactions, including friendships. It originates from disparities in viewpoints, attitudes, and expectations. Navigating conflict entails recognizing its presence, understanding its underlying reasons, and resolving it constructively to protect and improve relations. Conflict resolution is the act of handling conflicts and finding mutually acceptable solutions that meet the interests and concerns of all parties concerned.

Understanding Common Sources of Conflict in Friendships

Friendships can confront difficulties emanating from numerous causes, each bringing distinct challenges to the connection. Understanding these origins of conflict is key for properly addressing them. Common reasons of conflict in friendships include variations in communication styles, opposing interests or priorities, unresolved past difficulties, and changes in life circumstances. Additionally, misunderstandings, envy, and unmet expectations can also contribute to conflict. Recognizing these factors helps friends handle arguments with sensitivity and clarity.

Implementing Effective Conflict Resolution Strategies

Effective conflict resolution tactics enable friends to discuss disputes in a courteous, productive manner. These tactics include:

- *Open Communication:* Encourage open, honest discussion where both sides feel heard and understood. Active listening and expressing oneself without judgment improve understanding and empathy.

- *Empathy and Understanding*: Cultivate empathy by contemplating the other person's perspective and validating their emotions. Understanding the underlying sentiments and motives behind the disagreement might lead to greater settlement.

- *Finding Common Ground*: Identify similar aims and beliefs to develop common ground and encourage mutual understanding. Recognizing areas of agreement helps friends strive towards collaborative solutions.

- *Seeking Win-Win Solutions*: Collaborate to discover solutions that satisfy the requirements and concerns of both parties. By concentrating on mutual benefit, friends may sustain the connection while resolving dispute.

- *Taking Responsibility*: Acknowledge one's involvement in the disagreement and take responsibility for one's actions. Apologizing truly and making amends indicate accountability and a determination to mending the friendship.

- *Setting limits*: Establish clear limits to prevent future disagreements and safeguard the integrity of the connection. Respect for each other's limits builds trust and mutual respect.

By applying these conflict resolution tactics, friends may negotiate issues with grace and integrity, deepening their friendships and building deeper connections. Conflict, when managed well, offers a chance for growth, understanding, and enhanced resilience in friendships.

STEP 7
Prioritizing Time and Effort in Friendships

Friendships take conscious investment of time and effort to grow and thrive. In this chapter, we explore the importance of prioritizing friendships amidst other life commitments and the significance of spending time and effort in nurturing important relationships.

Balancing Friendships with Other Life Commitments

Friendships often fight with various other life commitments, including work, family responsibilities, and personal interests. Balancing these responsibilities requires conscious effort and planning to ensure that friendships receive the attention and care they deserve. While it's important to meet responsibilities in other areas of life, neglecting bonds can lead to feelings of isolation and disconnection. Finding a good balance involves setting limits, managing time effectively, and speaking freely with friends about competing goals.

Investing Time and Effort in Nurturing Meaningful Connections

Nurturing lasting connections takes conscious input of time, energy, and emotional support. It includes actively engaging in shared activities, fostering open conversation, and showing care and appreciation for one another. Investing in friendships goes beyond surface-level exchanges; it involves being present, supportive, and empathetic during both happy and difficult times. Friends who value time and effort in their interactions experience greater intimacy, trust, and happiness in their friendships.

Strategies for Prioritizing Time and Effort in Friendships

1. *Establishing Priorities*: Identify the bonds that hold the greatest importance in your life and rank them properly. Recognize the importance of keeping real connections amidst other tasks.

2. *Creating limits*: Set clear limits around your time and energy to prevent stress and overload. Communicate your limits to your friend and accept their lines as well.

3. *Scheduling Regular Check-ins*: Schedule regular check-ins or meet-ups with friends to stay linked and

strengthen the connection. Make time for great talks and shared events that strengthen your bond.

4. *Pay attention to them*: Pay attention by carefully engaging in conversations and showing real interest in your friend's experiences and feelings. Validate their thoughts and offer help when needed.

5. *Being Present*: Be fully present during encounters with friends, whether in person or online. Minimize distractions and focus on building real relationships in the moment.

6. *Showing Appreciation*: Express thanks and appreciation for your friends' presence in your life. Acknowledge their accomplishments, celebrate their wins, and offer support during difficult times.

By valuing time and effort in friendships, people develop stronger relationships, support networks, and sources of joy and satisfaction in their lives. Investing in important relationships enriches our experiences, strengthens our resilience, and enhances our general well-being.

STEP 8
Honouring Boundaries and Respect

Friendships grow in environments where limits are respected and respect is mutual. In this chapter, we delve into the value of setting healthy limits in friendships and respecting the boundaries of others.

Establishing Healthy Boundaries in Friendships

Healthy limits are important for keeping balance, trust, and mutual respect in friendships. They determine the boundaries of acceptable behaviour, personal space, and emotional support within the partnership. Establishing clear boundaries helps friends to express their wants, preferences, and limitations effectively. Healthy limits in friendships may include:

- *Communicating openly*: Expressing thoughts, feelings, and limits with honesty and clarity builds understanding and respect in friendships.

- *Setting limits*: Identifying personal limits and guidelines around time, space, and mental availability helps keep liberty and self-care within the friendship.

- ***Respecting differences:*** Acknowledging and respecting the varied views, values, and limits of friends cultivates understanding and empathy within the relationship.

- ***Being assertive***: Assertively asserting limits when they are broken or ignored reinforces mutual respect and fosters healthy communication in friendships.

- ***Practicing self-care***: Prioritizing self-care and well-being by setting limits around activities, responsibilities, and relationships encourages balance and resilience in friendships.

Respecting the Boundaries of Others

Respecting the limits of others is essential to growing trust, intimacy, and mutual respect in friendships. It includes honouring and validating the desires, boundaries, and autonomy of friends without judgment or pressure. Respecting the boundaries of others entails:

- ***Listening attentively***: Attentively listening to the needs, concerns, and limits of friends shows empathy and validation in the bond.

- *Asking for consent*: Seeking permission before sharing personal information, giving advice, or participating in physical touch shows respect for the rights and comfort of friends.

- *Being aware of triggers*: Sensitively recognizing and avoiding topics, activities, or behaviours that may trigger discomfort or distress in friends shows care and consideration for their well-being.

- *Offering support:* Providing emotional support, recognition, and encouragement in line with the limits and desires of friends promotes trust and security within the friendship.

- *Respecting confidentiality*: Upholding secrecy and respecting the privacy of friends by safeguarding shared information and experiences builds trust and loyalty in the friendship.

By observing limits and accepting the autonomy of others, friends create a safe, helpful, and caring environment where they can grow mentally and socially. Cultivating mutual respect and understanding creates stronger relationships, promotes mental well-being, and improves the quality and length of friendships

STEP 9
Celebrating Diversity and Inclusivity

Diversity and inclusivity are vital components of building important and enriching bonds. In this chapter, we explore the importance of praising difference and promoting tolerance within social groups.

Embracing Diversity in Friendships

Friendships grow in environments that embrace variety and respect the unique backgrounds, views, and experiences of people. Embracing difference in friendships involves:

- *Valuing differences*: Recognizing and respecting the varied cultural, ethnic, religious, and financial backgrounds of friends promotes mutual respect and understanding within the friendship.

- *Learning from each other*: Engaging in open conversation and carefully listening to friends' experiences and viewpoints promotes cross-cultural understanding and improves the bond with various views and insights.

- *Celebrating cultural traditions*: Embracing and sharing in each other's cultural traditions, festivals, and customs promotes equality and builds bonds of friendship.

- *Challenging biases and stereotypes*: Addressing biases and stereotypes within bonds develops understanding, kindness, and a dedication to social justice and equality.

Fostering Inclusivity and Acceptance in Your Social Circles

Creating inclusive and accepting social groups is important for creating a sense of connection and acceptance among friends. Fostering openness and acceptance involves:

- *Creating a safe space:* Establishing an environment where friends feel safe, respected, and valued promotes open conversation, openness, and trust within the social group.

- *Challenging exclusivity*: Addressing exclusivity and cliques within social circles supports inclusiveness and ensures that all members feel equally appreciated and included in group activities and talks.

- *Encouraging diverse perspectives*: Encouraging diverse perspectives and ideas within the social group encourages critical thought, creativity, and mutual respect among friends.

- Addressing discrimination and prejudice: Confronting discrimination and prejudice within social groups encourages responsibility, understanding, and a dedication to creating a more fair and inclusive society.

- Supporting marginalized views: Amplifying the opinions and experiences of marginalized people within the social group encourages understanding, unity, and social change.

By praising diversity and supporting equality within social groups, friends create a helpful, polite, and rewarding environment where individuals feel valuable, accepted, and empowered to express their true selves. Prioritizing diversity and equality in friendships supports empathy, understanding, and social cohesion, eventually strengthening the bonds of friendship and building a more inclusive society.

STEP 10
Sustaining Long-Term Friendships

Friendships have the potential to endure and improve our lives over the long term, provided we develop and support them with care and intentionality. In this chapter, we explore methods for fostering resilience, adaptability, and mutual support to promote lifelong relationships.

Cultivating Resilience and Adaptability in Friendships

Friendships, like any connection, face challenges and changes over time. Cultivating resilience and adaptability allows us to handle these natural ups and downs with grace and understanding. Strategies for developing grit and flexibility include:

- *Open communication*: Maintaining open, honest communication helps friends to address challenges, voice concerns, and work through problems together.

- *Flexibility*: Remaining flexible and open-minded in the face of changes or disagreements helps friends adapt to changing conditions and maintain the strength of their bond.

- *Problem-solving skills*: Developing effective problem-solving skills allows friends to cooperate, compromise, and find helpful answers to problems or disagreements.

- *Acceptance of change*: Embracing the truth of change and shift in friendships promotes resiliency and equips friends to manage life's transitions with grace and understanding.

Nurturing Lifelong Connections through Mutual Support and Understanding

Lifelong relationships are built on a base of mutual support, understanding, and shared experiences. Nurturing these connections takes ongoing work, empathy, and dedication. Strategies for nurturing lasting ties include:

- *Providing constant support*: Offering unwavering support, encouragement, and understanding during both happy and difficult times strengthens the ties of friendship and creates a sense of security and trust.

- *Listening*: Engaging in active listening and showing empathy and understanding towards friends' experiences and feelings improves mutual connection and creates emotional closeness.

- *praising milestones*: Acknowledging and praising milestones, successes, and shared experiences strengthens the value and importance of the bond, creating lasting memories and strengthening emotional ties.

- *Prioritizing quality time*: Investing time and energy in meaningful exchanges, shared activities, and quality talks strengthens the bonds of friendship and cultivates a sense of belonging and connection.

By fostering resilience, flexibility, and mutual support, friends can sustain and nurture lasting relationships that bring joy, satisfaction, and friendship to their lives

Conclusion
Embracing the Journey of Friendship

In the study of friendship, we have delved into the intricacies and nuances that define real relationships between people. Throughout this trip, we have discovered the essence of true friendship, traversed the terrain of understanding and empathy, and navigated the challenges and joys that accompany contributing to lasting bonds.

Friendship is a dynamic and evolving part of human experience, weaving its threads through the fabric of our lives and forming our sense of identity, connection, and satisfaction. It is a journey marked by times of laughter and tears, celebration and comfort, growth and change.

At its core, friendship is built on a base of sincerity, trust, and mutual respect. It grows in the rich soil of empathy, understanding, and acceptance, where people can easily express themselves and be met with kindness and support.

Throughout our study, we have found that true friendships transcend barriers of space, time, and situation. They are sustained by the shared experiences, cherished memories, and unwavering commitment of those who start on the trip together.

As we reflect on the parts of this journey, we recognize the importance of accepting variety, respecting limits, and managing disagreements with kindness and understanding. We enjoy the beauty and depth that diversity brings to our bonds, supporting tolerance, acceptance, and mutual respect in our social groups.

In developing lifelong relationships, we foster endurance, adaptability, and mutual support, anchoring ourselves in the warmth and stability of enduring links. Through active listening, empathy, and meaningful conversation, we improve our connections and strengthen the ties that bind us together.

As we finish our study of friendship, let us carry forward the lessons learned and the insights gained into our interactions and relationships

In the fabric of life, friendship is the thread that binds us together, creating a mosaic of love, fun, and shared experiences. As we move ahead, may the bonds of friendship guide us, support us, and improve our lives in ways both deep and enduring.

WRITER EMAIL ADDRESS

Patiencejohn141@gmail.com

THE END